Daily
Activity
Bank

Editorial Offices: Glenview, Illinois • Parsippany, New Jersey • New York, New York
Sales Offices: Parsippany, New Jersey • Duluth, Georgia • Glenview, Illinois • Coppell, Texas • Ontario, California

www.sfsocialstudies.com

Contents

ISBN 0-328-03921-7

2 3 4 5 6 7 8 9 10 V008 10 09 08 07 06 05 04 03 02

Fast Fact 1

Dover, Delaware; Honolulu, Hawaii; Indianapolis, Indiana; and Oklahoma City, Oklahoma, are the four United States capital cities that begin with the same letter as the state in which they are located.

What is the capital city of your state, and where is it located?

Geography

History

Fast Fact 2

President Grover Cleveland had an artificial jaw made of rubber.

What is one other fact you can find about Grover Cleveland?

Fast Fact 3

The smallest money ever used was called an *obelas.* It was used in Greece and was smaller than an apple seed!

What is the smallest size coin that we use today?

Economics

Government
Citizenship

Fast Fact 4

American flags should never touch the ground.

What does the American flag mean to you?

Fast Fact 5

Do you like pancakes? Mexican tortillas, Chinese Mandarin rolls, and French crepes are all different kinds of pancakes.

What do you think Native Americans ground and used for pancakes?

Culture

Geography

Fast Fact 6

The Great Barrier Reef is the largest coral reef in the world. It stretches for 1,250 miles in the Coral Sea.

The Great Barrier Reef is located off what continent?

Fast Fact 7

Pocahontas's real name was Matoaka. Pocahontas, a Powhatan, encouraged peace between her people and the English colonists.

Why was it important for the Powhatans and the colonists to get along?

History

Economics

Fast Fact 8

President Ronald Reagan loved jelly beans so much that his frequent eating of the candies increased their sales during his presidency.

What can cause a product to become popular?

Fast Fact 9

In 1904 Mary McLeod Bethune began a school for African American girls in Daytona, Florida. At first, there were five students who used boxes for desks. The school later became a college.

Why might it have been hard for an African American girl to get a good education in 1904?

Government Citizenship

Culture

Fast Fact 10

It is an American tradition for the President to throw out the first ball at the start of each new baseball season.

How many professional baseball teams can you name? Name them.

Fast Fact 11

The United States Geological Survey has been making maps of the United States since 1879.

Why might new maps be needed?

Geography

History

Fast Fact 12

Pioneers traveling west called their wagons "prairie schooners" because, from a distance, the white wagon covers made the wagons look like ships, or schooners.

What things might pioneers have packed in their wagons for the long trip west?

Fast Fact 13

Different values of money are called denominations. Paper money is all the same size and color and each denomination has a different portrait of a famous American on it.

Whose portrait is on a $1 bill? Whose portrait is on a $5 bill?

Economics

Government Citizenship

Fast Fact 14

Oliver Wendell Holmes was the oldest justice to have served on the Supreme Court. He retired at the age of 90.

What does the Supreme Court do?

Fast Fact 15

The Chinese give each new year the name of an animal, such as monkey or tiger. The year of the rabbit is said to be a very lucky year.

What animal would you choose as a name for a new year? Why?

Culture

Geography

Fast Fact 16

Russia is the world's largest country in size.

Russia touches what two continents?

Fast Fact 17

It took more than 14 years to carve the statues of Presidents George Washington, Thomas Jefferson, Abraham Lincoln, and Theodore Roosevelt into the mountain at Mount Rushmore.

In what state is Mount Rushmore located?

History

Economics

Fast Fact 18

Tobacco was used as money in and around Virginia for almost 100 years.

How might you have gotten the things you needed to live if you did not have tobacco to use as money?

Fast Fact 19

The Statue of Freedom on top of the United States Capitol stands 19'6" tall and weighs almost 15,000 pounds.

Where is the United States Capitol located, and why is it important?

Government Citizenship

Culture

Fast Fact 20

Many children in Vietnam celebrate the beauty of the October full moon by carrying lanterns that light up the night, wearing masks, and eating moon cakes. This festival is called Trung Thu.

What holidays do you celebrate in the fall?

Fast Fact 21

The first steel-frame skyscraper was built in Chicago in 1885. It was only ten stories high!

To reach Chicago from Philadelphia, what direction would you travel?

Geography

History

Fast Fact 22

On December 17, 1903, the Wright brothers had the first successful flight in a heavier-than-air powered airplane.

Where did this flight take place?

Fast Fact 23

Chicago's central business district is called the *Loop* because of the elevated train tracks that circle the area.

Why is a passenger train helpful near the business district of a large city?

Economics

Government Citizenship

Fast Fact 24

During the 1920s driving became an important leisure activity. People took drives in the countryside, but lack of road signs often caused problems!

Make a quick list of all of the road signs you can think of.

Fast Fact 25

The most popular sport in South America is soccer.

Describe how someone who plays soccer—or a different sport—scores.

Culture

Geography

Fast Fact 26

The equator passes through six countries on the continent of Africa.

What are the names of these six countries?

Fast Fact 27

Our national song, "The Star-Spangled Banner," was written as a poem in 1814. Soon the poem was set to music.

How would you name and describe other symbols of our nation?

History

Economics

Fast Fact 28

Paul Revere's metals company once supplied the United States Mint with rolled copper for the production of early cents.

Draw the front and back of a penny. How many details can you remember?

Fast Fact 29

For a long time in this country, women were not allowed to vote. But that didn't stop Susan B. Anthony from voting for President in 1872. She was arrested, and a judge said she had to pay a fine of $100.

Why do you think that Susan B. Anthony refused to pay the fine?

Government Citizenship

Culture

Fast Fact 30

The Aloha Festival, Hawaii's largest festival, is a celebration of Hawaii's music, dance, and history. The Aloha Festival lasts for two months.

How would you describe a special celebration that takes place in your state?

Fast Fact 31

The Komodo dragon is the largest lizard in the world. These lizards live on the island of Komodo in Indonesia and eat deer, pigs, and even water buffalo!

What is the name of another island that is part of Indonesia?

Geography

History

Fast Fact 32

At the age of 69, President Ronald Reagan was the oldest President to be inaugurated.

What are the advantages of having an older person hold an important job such as President?

Fast Fact 33

Madam C. J. Walker became the first African American female millionaire by making hair care products for African Americans.

How many zeros do you write when you write one million?

Economics

Government
Citizenship

Fast Fact 34

The United States is mostly a nation of immigrants, or people who left their home country looking for a better life. For that reason, the United States is often called the "melting pot."

Tell about someone you know, or have read about, whose family came to the United States from another country.

Fast Fact 35

Each January, for more than 100 years, St. Paul, Minnesota, has held an outdoor winter carnival featuring a huge ice castle. This is a cool celebration!

What can you tell about a celebration in your town or city?

Culture

Geography

Fast Fact 36

Vatican City is the smallest country in the world! It is located within the city of Rome.

Where would you travel to visit Vatican City?

Fast Fact 37

King Henry the Eighth of England married six times. Three of his wives were named Catherine, two were named Anne, and one was named Jane.

What is a king? What is a queen?

History

Economics

Since 1965 there have been no silver dimes and quarters. Since 1970 there has been no silver in the United States "silver" dollar.

Why do you think the United States Mint stopped using silver to make coins?

Fast Fact 39

In colonial times, the "town crier" announced important news to keep the people informed.

What are four ways people learn of important news today?

Government
Citizenship

Culture

Fast Fact 40

Eskimo is the name Europeans gave Inuits. Traditionally Inuits lived in tents in the summer and wood and sod huts in the winter.

What materials are used to build homes near you?

Fast Fact 41

Angel Falls, located in Venezuela, is the tallest waterfall in the world. It is 3,212 feet high.

Where is Venezuela located?

Geography

History

Fast Fact 42

Andrew Jackson was the first President to be born in a log cabin.

When and where were you born?

Fast Fact 43

After being rejected by 29 medical schools because she was a woman, Elizabeth Blackwell was accepted at Geneva College in 1848. Later she started her own medical school.

People go to college to study for what other jobs?

Economics

Government
Citizenship

Fast Fact 44

The first two political parties in America were the Federalists and the Antifederalists.

What are the two main political parties today?

Fast Fact 45

Many different groups of people live in Africa. The Watusis in Burundi are among the tallest people in the world; adult men are often more than 7 feet tall. Men of the Pygmy tribe of the Democratic Republic of the Congo are often less than 5 feet tall.

What would be good and bad about being either very tall or very short?

Culture

Geography

Fast Fact 46

Four Corners is the spot where the states of Utah, Colorado, Arizona, and New Mexico meet. You can place your two hands and two feet so that you can be in four different states at the same time!

Find these four states on a map and name the capital of each.

Fast Fact 47

Spanish explorers founded St. Augustine, Florida, in 1565, more than 400 years ago.

Look on a map. What might you see if you visited St. Augustine today?

History

Economics

Fast Fact 48

Beginning in 1896, most farmers could get their mail delivered every day. Farm families often used mail order catalogs to order their clothing and household goods.

Why are mail order catalogs still used today?

Fast Fact 49

Relationships with other countries are called foreign affairs.

Why does America want to have good relationships with other countries?

Government Citizenship

Culture

Fast Fact 50

During Ramadan, Muslim people do not eat or drink from sunrise to sunset for an entire month. At the end of Ramadan, Muslims celebrate with a festival.

Share religious traditions with which you may be familiar.

Fast Fact 51

Who turned off Niagara Falls? In 1848 ice chunks blocked the Niagara River, and Niagara Falls came to a stop for 40 hours.

Which two Great Lakes are connected by Niagara Falls?

Geography

History

Fast Fact 52

Christopher Columbus landed on a Caribbean Island called Quisqueya, not the continent of North America, in 1492.

Name another European explorer of the Americas. Where did he come from, and where did he go?

Fast Fact 53

Canada has a $1.00 coin that pictures a loon, a kind of water bird. These coins are called "loonies"! Canadian $2.00 coins are called "toonies"!

What denominations of coins do we use in the United States?

Economics

Government Citizenship

Fast Fact 54

President Theodore Roosevelt made the "White House" the official name of the President's home. It used to be called the "President's House" or the "Executive Mansion."

Besides the White House, what other important sights can you see in Washington, D.C.?

Fast Fact 55

The words *coffee* and *sugar* come from the Arabic words *kahwa* and *sokkhar*.

What other English words do you know that have been borrowed from another language?

Culture

Geography

Fast Fact 56

The Rio Grande is 1,885 miles long. This river begins in Colorado and empties into the Gulf of Mexico.

Between what two countries does the Rio Grande form a border?

Fast Fact 57

Louis Joliet was a Canadian who explored the Mississippi River.

Name another person who explored the middle of the continent of North America.

History

Economics

Fast Fact 58

The ice cream that you see in advertisements isn't really ice cream! It is a mixture of vegetable shortening, corn syrup, and confectioner's sugar that won't melt under the photographer's hot lights.

How do advertisements affect the demand for a product like ice cream?

Fast Fact 59

Did you know that it is against the law to slurp your soup in a restaurant in New Jersey?

Why do we have laws?

Government
Citizenship

Culture

Fast Fact 60

On the Day of the Dead, a Mexican holiday that honors loved ones who have died, people eat sugar skulls as treats.

What special foods are used to celebrate holidays that you know about?

Fast Fact 61

Mount Everest, located in the Himalayas near Nepal, is the highest point in the world. It is 29,028 feet above sea level.

What is the highest point in the United States?

Geography

History

Fast Fact 62

In England in the 1300s, people's last names often identified the job they did. A stoneworker's last name would be Stone. A person who cut hair would have the last name of Barber.

What names can you think of that might tell what someone's ancestors did for a living?

Fast Fact 63

If you save 50¢ every school day starting in third grade, you will have about $900 dollars when you graduate from high school.

What categories should you include when you make a budget?

Economics

Government Citizenship

Fast Fact 64

In 1893 New Zealand became the first country in the world to give women the right to vote.

Who can vote in the United States today?

Fast Fact 65

In Europe, people eat holding their forks in their left hands and their knives in their right hands.

What other cultural differences between the United States and other countries do you know?

Culture

Geography

Fast Fact 66

Monarch butterflies fly about 1,500 miles from their birthplaces in the northeastern United States to Mexico for the winter!

Pick a place in Mexico. About how far would you have to travel from your home to get there?

Fast Fact 67

The marathon, a 26.2-mile race, is named after a Greek hero named Pheidippedes. He ran about 26 miles to Athens to announce that the Greeks had won the Battle of Marathon. As soon as he announced the victory, he dropped dead!

The marathon is an Olympic event. What other Olympic events do you know about?

History

Economics

Fast Fact 68

In 1273 a Mongolian emperor invented paper money. Why? His tax collectors and their horses were collapsing from carrying heavy sacks of coins!

What are some ways people today can pay for things, other than with coins or paper money?

Fast Fact 69

Vexillology is the study of flags and their history.

What do the stars and stripes on the United States flag stand for?

Government Citizenship

Culture

Fast Fact 70

A tartan is a plaid, woolen cloth. There are nearly 3,000 kinds of tartans. Different tartans represent different districts, clans, and families in Scotland.

Can you think of areas of our country or of other countries that are associated with a particular kind of clothing?

Fast Fact 71

Deserts cover one-fifth of the land surface of the world.

Name a desert near the African country of Mali.

Geography

History

Fast Fact 72

People from Oklahoma are called "Sooners" because they claimed their land sooner than they were supposed to. The Oklahoma Territory wasn't officially open for settlement then.

Do people in your state or region have a nickname? What is it?

Fast Fact 73

The motto on the first United States penny, minted in 1787, was "Mind your business."

What mottos are written on pennies, nickels, and dimes that are used today?

Economics

Government Citizenship

Fast Fact 74

After Texas became a state in 1845, Sam Houston became one of the United States senators from Texas. He later became the governor of Texas!

Who is the current governor of your state?

Fast Fact 75

The Sears Tower in Chicago is 110 stories high.

What famous skyscrapers do you know about? Where are they located?

Culture

Geography

Fast Fact 76

Toronto is a Native American word that most likely meant "place of meeting."

Why do you think Native Americans might have chosen Toronto, which is now a city in Canada, as a meeting place?

Fast Fact 77

In the late 1800s, Andrew Carnegie made his fortune by making steel. In 1900 he was the richest man in the world.

What things that you use every day are made of steel?

History

Economics

Fast Fact 78

Does your money glow? If it's real, it should. New $20 bills have a thread in them that glows in ultraviolet light.

Why does the government make money difficult to copy?

Fast Fact 79

President Franklin Delano Roosevelt was the only person to be elected President four times.

Who is the current United States President?
Who is the Vice-President?

Government Citizenship

Culture

Fast Fact 80

In the mid-1800s, Amelia Jenks Bloomer shocked her community by wearing loose-fitting pants in public. Back then women wore long dresses or skirts. The pants were named "bloomers" after her.

How have styles of dress changed for women from the 1800s to today?

Fast Fact 81

North America is the third largest continent.

What are the names of the seven continents?

Geography

History

Fast Fact 82

In 1881 Clara Barton began the American branch of the Red Cross.

What does the Red Cross do?

Fast Fact 83

A survey of about 1,000 children across the country showed that 43 percent received an allowance, 26 percent received some spending money, and the rest received no money at all.

What lessons can you learn from having an allowance?

Economics

Government Citizenship

Fast Fact 84

In colonial times some places in New England used the "corn and bean" voting method. A kernel of corn stood for one candidate, a bean for the other!

What system of voting do you use in classroom or school elections?

Fast Fact 85

Nguba is an African word for "peanut," and Africans brought peanuts to Georgia. Peanuts are called "goobers" in Georgia.

What other foods that we enjoy today were brought from other countries?

Culture

Geography

Fast Fact 86

The capital of our country was originally to be called "Columbia" after Christopher Columbus. Instead it was named after George Washington.

What does the "D.C." in Washington, D.C., stand for?

Fast Fact 87

The walls of Castillo de San Marcos in St. Augustine, Florida, are made of coquina, a stone made up of tiny seashells. Enemy cannonballs would either bounce off or sink into the coquina walls!

What are houses and other buildings made of where you live?

History

Economics

Fast Fact 88

If your paper money gets torn or damaged, don't worry! As long as you have more than half of the bill, you can exchange it at a bank for a new bill.

What are some other services that banks provide?

Fast Fact 89

In Italy small balls of different colors were used to cast secret votes. Our word *ballot* comes from the Italian word for "little ball," *ballotta.*

What is a secret ballot?

Government
Citizenship

Culture

Fast Fact 90

For hundreds of years the game of lacrosse was the favorite sport of Native Americans in the United States and Canada.

What sports are popular in our culture today?

Fast Fact 91

There are at least 20 times as many sheep as there are people in New Zealand!

Is New Zealand in the Northern Hemisphere or the Southern Hemisphere?

Geography

History

Fast Fact 92

The Brooklyn Bridge, a New York City landmark, was the longest suspension bridge in the country when it opened in 1883.

What historic landmarks can be found in your community?

Fast Fact 93

Before the American Revolution, colonists used English money—pounds sterling, shillings, and pence.

What countries today use the *peso* as money?

Economics

Government
Citizenship

Fast Fact 94

In 1861 Congress passed the first income tax in the United States.

What is a tax that even third-graders pay?

Fast Fact 95

The words *moose, muskrat, caribou, skunk,* and *opossum* are all Native American words.

Look at a map and find names of places in our country that came from Native American words.

Culture

Geography

Fast Fact 96

Water covers 70 percent of the Earth's surface.

What are the names of the four oceans?

Fast Fact 97

In the late 1800s, the United States Army tried using bicycles instead of horses. Too many flat tires convinced the army to keep the horses!

What are other branches of the United States military besides the Army?

History

Economics

Fast Fact 98

The average coin lasts for about 25 years.

What does a mint have to do with coins?

Fast Fact 99

The teddy bear is named after President Theodore Roosevelt, whose nickname was Teddy.

How many past Presidents can you name? Name them.

Government Citizenship

Culture

Fast Fact 100

Boxing Day is a British holiday celebrated on December 26. People give money and gifts, traditionally in boxes, to needy people.

What is a holiday that you know about that is celebrated in a different country or in a different region of this country?

Fast Fact 101

There are 24 standard time zones on Earth. When it is noon in New York, New York, it is 9 A.M. in Los Angeles, California.

In what time zone of the United States do you live?

Geography

History

Fast Fact 102

In 1981 Sandra Day O'Connor became the first woman appointed as a justice of the Supreme Court.

How many justices does the Supreme Court of the United States have?

Fast Fact 103

In 2002 the twelve countries in the European Union began using the *euro,* a new standard unit of money. Now all the countries in the European Union will use the same money.

Look at a map of Europe. Why do you think these countries decided to use one common kind of money?

Economics

Government Citizenship

Fast Fact 104

The Twenty-second Amendment to the United States Constitution says that no President can be elected to office for more than two terms.

How many terms has the current President served?

Fast Fact 105

Every May 5 children in Japan celebrate Children's Day, a holiday to honor children.

List all of the holidays you can think of that are celebrated in the United States. Which one is your favorite?

Culture

Geography

Fast Fact 106

The Nile River, which runs through Egypt and Sudan, is the longest river in the world. It is 4,160 miles long.

What rivers are in your region of the United States?

Fast Fact 107

During the Gold Rush in 1849, the population of California grew from 20,000 people to more than 100,000 people!

What is the name of the capital of California, which is located near where the Gold Rush began?

History

Economics

Fast Fact 108

Automobiles are a major export of the United States. They are also a major import!

What countries export cars to the United States?

Fast Fact 109

At one time Michigan had a law making it illegal to hitch a crocodile to a fire hydrant!

What laws must you obey when you are riding a bicycle?

Government Citizenship

Culture

Fast Fact 110

The street names in the game Monopoly® are real streets in Atlantic City, New Jersey.

What are some other popular board games that you like to play?

Fast Fact 111

The state of Arkansas has a working diamond mine.

About how far is it from your state to Arkansas?

Geography

History

Fast Fact 112

Ronald Reagan was an actor before he became the United States President in 1981, and Dwight D. Eisenhower was a career Army officer before he became President in 1953.

What did the current President of the United States do before he took office?

Fast Fact 113

October 29, 1929, is known as Black Tuesday. It was the day the New York Stock Exchange crashed.

Where can you look to find the current value of a stock?

Economics

Government
Citizenship

Fast Fact 114

Yellowstone National Park was the first national park. It was established in 1872.

In what three states is Yellowstone National Park located?

Fast Fact 115

The first color TV program was broadcast in 1951.

What inventions in home entertainment have become available since 1951?

Culture

Geography

Fast Fact 116

Seven American Presidents were born in Ohio.

What states border Ohio?

Fast Fact 117

Until 1932 a first-class postage stamp cost only 2¢.

What does a first-class stamp cost today?

History

Economics

Fast Fact 118

Of all the states, California and Texas earn the most money from farming.

Why do you think this is so?

Fast Fact 119

A baby who is born in the United States is automatically a United States citizen.

What are the responsibilities of good citizenship?

Government Citizenship

Culture

Fast Fact 120

From 1880 to 1950 Mary was the most popular name for a girl born in the United States.

What is the most popular name in your class? in your grade? in your school?

Fast Fact 121

Eight Presidents were born in Virginia—more than in any other state.

What states border Virginia?

Geography

History

Fast Fact 122

By 1889 the great herds of 60 million bison that had once roamed the Great Plains were reduced to fewer than 1,000 animals.

What is another word for *bison*? Describe a bison.

Fast Fact 123

Superman first appeared in the June 1938 issue of *Action Comics*. That issue is now worth $180,000!

What makes an item like a comic book so valuable?

Economics

Government
Citizenship

Fast Fact 124

In 1904 in New York State the maximum speed limit for cars was 20 miles per hour.

Speed limits are set to help prevent accidents. What other laws have been passed to keep drivers and passengers safe?

Fast Fact 125

In 1884 the first roller coaster was opened at an amusement park in Coney Island in New York. It was called the *Switchback*.

What amusement parks have you heard about or visited? What are some attractions at those parks?

Culture

Geography

Fast Fact 126

The state of Florida has more than 800 miles of sandy coastline!

Name a Florida city that is on the Atlantic side of the state and one that is on the Gulf of Mexico side.

Fast Fact 127

On February 12, 1909, the NAACP was founded in the United States. One of the founders was an educator named W. E. B. Du Bois.

What do the initials NAACP stand for?

History

Economics

Fast Fact 128

Bananas are a tropical fruit. India and Brazil both grow millions of tons of bananas every year.

Are bananas an export or an import in the United States?

Fast Fact 129

Whenever the President of the United States, current or former, arrives or leaves an event, he is entitled to a 21-gun salute.

Why might the President and Vice-President choose not to take advantage of this honor?

Government Citizenship

Culture

Fast Fact 130

Steamboat Willie, **the first animated cartoon with sound, opened in a theater in New York in 1928. The cartoon starred Mickey Mouse.**

What cartoons and cartoon characters are popular today?

Fast Fact 131

The Appalachian Trail is a 2,100-mile hiking path through the Appalachian Mountains. You can hike from Maine to Georgia in about six months.

What are the names of three other states that the Appalachian Mountains extend through?

Geography

History

Fast Fact 132

The Panama Canal, which joins the Atlantic and the Pacific Oceans, was completed in 1914.

What countries border the country of Panama?

Fast Fact 133

In 1950 the Diners Club card was issued in the United States. It was the first credit card.

What does *credit* mean? How does a credit card work?

Economics

Fast Fact 134

At the end of the twentieth century, Richard M. Nixon was the only President to have resigned from office.

Who takes over the job of President if the President dies or, like Nixon, resigns?

Fast Fact 135

In 1974 the first triathlon was held in the United States. It is a sporting event that combines bicycling, running, and swimming in one competition.

What sports can people participate in in your community?

Culture

Fast Fact 136

There is an official list of names for six years worth of hurricanes! And then the list is reused. So we already know that the first hurricane of 2009 will be named Ana, and the second one will be named Bill!

Hurricanes are natural disasters. What other natural disasters happen in the world?

Fast Fact 137

The Golden Gate Bridge, a suspension bridge in California, opened in 1937.

What body of water does the Golden Gate Bridge cross?

History

Economics

Fast Fact 138

In the United States April 15 is the date when people must file their income tax returns and pay their income taxes.

What are some things that taxes help pay for?

Fast Fact 139

Who is Uncle Sam, anyway? No one is sure of the origin of Uncle Sam, the tall, bearded man who is a symbol of the United States and its people.

What are some other symbols of the United States?

Government Citizenship

Culture

Fast Fact 140

In 1913 the first modern crossword puzzle was printed in a New York city newspaper.

What entertainment features does your newspaper include in its pages?

Fast Fact 141

The Mammoth Cave system in the United States is the longest cave system in the world.

What state would you have to visit to tour Mammoth Cave?

Geography

History

Fast Fact 142

Nelson Mandela, South Africa's first black president, was awarded the Nobel Peace Prize, named after Alfred Nobel.

Who was Mr. Nobel?

Fast Fact 143

The federal minimum hourly wage was $0.75 per hour in 1950. Fifty years later it was $5.15 per hour.

When you are old enough to start working, how would you like to earn a wage?

Economics

Government Citizenship

Fast Fact 144

The first census of the United States was taken in 1790. Census takers rode through the states on horseback to conduct the census.

How is the census conducted now?

Fast Fact 145

Would you believe that Paul Bunyan, the mythical lumberjack, dug the Grand Canyon? Tall tales in the West tell how he did it!

In what state is the Grand Canyon?

Culture

Geography

Fast Fact 146

The state of Hawaii is made up entirely of islands—more than 120 of them!

How would you describe the geography of your state?

Fast Fact 147

United States Air Force Captain Charles E. Yeager broke the sound barrier in 1947. He flew faster than the speed of sound in his rocket plane.

What achievements has the United States made in the exploration of space?

History

Economics

Fast Fact 148

In 2001 American Dennis Tito paid the Russian government $20 million to join the Russian crew on a trip to the International Space Station.

Did Mr. Tito purchase goods or services from the Russians?

Fast Fact 149

The Liberty Bell was rung on July 8, 1776, for the first public reading of the Declaration of Independence.

From whom did our country's founders declare independence?

Government Citizenship

Culture

Fast Fact 150

English is the third most widely spoken language in the world.

What are some countries where English is spoken?

Fast Fact 151

Tokyo, Japan, is the most populous city in the world. The Tokyo metropolitan area is home to more than 30 million people.

What is the population of your city or town?

Geography

History

Fast Fact 152

In 1871 the Great Chicago Fire destroyed 17,450 buildings and killed 250 people.

In what state is the city of Chicago?

Fast Fact 153

The United States Mint is releasing a new quarter, from 1999 through 2008, for every state. Each state gets to design its own quarter.

Whose portrait is on every quarter?

Economics

Government Citizenship

Fast Fact 154

In the 1900s Alice Stebbins joined the Los Angeles police department. She was one of the world's first women police officers.

What is the job of a police officer?

Fast Fact 155

The state of Tennessee has five state songs! They are "My Homeland, Tennessee," "When It's Iris Time in Tennessee," "My Tennessee," "Tennessee Waltz," and "Rocky Top."

Name the capital of Tennessee, which is also the center of country music.

Culture

Geography

Fast Fact 156

Both China and India have populations greater than one billion people!

On what continent are the countries of China and India?

Fast Fact 157

"We Shall Overcome" became the song of the civil rights movement in the 1960s.

Rosa Parks was one of the leaders of the civil rights movement. What is she famous for doing?

History

Economics

Fast Fact 158

Farmers did not want to gamble on Cyrus McCormick's reaper. It took him seven years to make his first sale!

What does a reaper do?

Fast Fact 159

The justices of the Supreme Court have a tradition in which each justice shakes hands with the other eight judges before going into the courtroom or before beginning private conferences.

Where is the Supreme Court located?

Government Citizenship

Culture

Fast Fact 160

About 80 percent of Internet users use e-mail.

What does the *e* in *e-mail* stand for?

Fast Fact 161

Canada and the United States share the world's longest border—about 4,000 miles!

Which of the Great Lakes lies entirely within the border of the United States?

Geography

History

Fast Fact 162

Early Ford cars were known as "Tin Lizzies." Over 15 million of them were sold!

Who was Henry Ford, and what is he known for?

Fast Fact 163

Levi Strauss invented blue jeans in 1853 to meet the needs of the gold miners in California during the Gold Rush. He made them of sturdy denim.

Why were Strauss's blue jeans a success?

Economics

Fast Fact 164

New York's Central Park, which covers more than 700 acres in the middle of Manhattan, was designed by Frederick Law Olmstead.

What does a park district do?

Fast Fact 165

The Smithsonian Institution in Washington, D.C., is the world's largest museum complex—it includes 16 museums and art galleries, as well as the National Zoo.

What museums, zoos, or other educational institutions are located near where you live?

Culture

Geography

Fast Fact 166

A ship can travel 2,342 miles from the Atlantic Ocean all the way to Duluth, Minnesota, by sailing on the Great Lakes and through the locks on the St. Lawrence Seaway.

What kind of locks would you find on a seaway?

Fast Fact 167

Many cowboys in the mid-1800s were Mexican and African American. Mexican cowboys were known as *vaqueros*.

What is a cattle drive?

History

Economics

Fast Fact 168

Billboard advertising became popular in the early 1900s.

How does advertising affect the sale of goods and services?

Fast Fact 169

There is nothing in the United States Constitution about a Cabinet, but every President since George Washington has had one.

What is the Cabinet?

Government Citizenship

Culture

Fast Fact 170

Boston was the first city in the United States to build a subway.

What is a subway?

Fast Fact 171

Aloha! Hawaii became the 50th state of the United States in 1959.

What state is closest to Hawaii?

Geography

History

Fast Fact 172

Early settlers on the Great Plains lived in "soddies," houses made of sod, which are pieces of ground covered with grass.

What building materials were used to build your school?

Fast Fact 173

Early movie theaters were called nickelodeons because the price of admission was a nickel!

How much does it cost to see a movie in a theater today? Does everyone pay the same price?

Economics

Government
Citizenship

Fast Fact 174

The United States is working with Brazil, Canada, Italy, Japan, Russia, and ten other European nations to build a manned space station.

NASA is our federal agency in charge of this project. What does NASA stand for?

Fast Fact 175

Smile! Color film was introduced in the United States in 1937.

What are some improvements in photography since 1937?

Culture

Geography

Fast Fact 176

Adobe, a mixture of sun-dried clay and straw, is used to build houses in the Southwest.

What is the name of a state in the Southwest?

Fast Fact 177

World War I, which ended in 1918, was called "the war to end all wars."

What other wars has the United States been involved in since World War I?

History

Economics

Fast Fact 178

Coins from ancient Athens, Greece, pictured an owl. The owl was for Athena, the goddess of wisdom.

What bird is pictured on some United States coins?

Fast Fact 179

Early United States citizens could not say the "Pledge of Allegiance." It wasn't written until 1892!

What does the word *allegiance* mean?

Government Citizenship

Culture

Fast Fact 180

Americans loved their cars and the movies in the 1950s. Drive-in movies allowed them to enjoy both at the same time!

Where do people watch movies today?

Fast Facts Answers

1. Anwers will vary from state to state.
2. Grover Cleveland was born in 1837 in New Jersey and was both our 22nd and 24th President. He is the only President to have served two nonconsecutive terms.
3. The dime is the smallest in size.
4. Answers will vary but may include that the flag is a symbol of our country and freedom.
5. acorns or corn, also called maize
6. Australia
7. Answers may include that the Powhatans and colonists were living in the same area and the colonists needed the Powhatans' help in learning how to survive in the new land. The Powhatans helped the colonists find food and grow crops.
8. Answers may include that it is well advertised; it is new or different; and famous people are seen buying or using it.
9. In many areas of the country, black children and white children attended separate schools. Often the schools black children attended were not as good as the schools white children attended. Some people thought education was more important for boys than for girls.
10. Answers may include the Baltimore Orioles, San Francisco Giants, Detroit Tigers, Cleveland Indians, Boston Red Sox, New York Mets, Arizona Diamondbacks, Seattle Mariners, San Diego Padres, Los Angeles Dodgers, New York Yankees, St. Louis Cardinals, Houston Astros, Pittsburg Pirates, Philadelphia Phillies, Kansas City Royals, or others.
11. Answers may include that the names of streets, towns, or even countries change; boundaries change; lakes may dry up or the course of rivers may change; and new information becomes available.
12. Answers will vary but may include food, clothing, cooking utensils, furniture, and tools.

13. George Washington, Abraham Lincoln
14. Answers may include that the Supreme Court hears cases about local, state, and national laws; the Supreme Court is the highest court in the land; Supreme Court judges use the Constitution as a guide when deciding cases.
15. Answers will vary.
16. Asia and Europe
17. South Dakota
18. Answers may include making or growing what you needed to live; bartering; finding something else of value to use as money.
19. Washington, D.C.; Answers may include that Congress meets in the Capitol; the Capitol is an important landmark; it is a symbol of our government.
20. Answers will vary but may include Halloween and Thanksgiving.
21. west
22. near Kitty Hawk, North Carolina
23. It brings workers to their jobs, and it moves people within the business district.
24. Answers will include some of the following signs: speed limit, no passing, stop, train crossing, curve ahead, road names or route numbers, caution, animal crossing.
25. Soccer players score by knocking the ball into a net cage at either end of the field. Answers should be correct for the other sports named.
26. Gabon, Republic of the Congo, Democratic Republic of the Congo, Uganda, Kenya, Somalia
27. Answers may include the bald eagle, the rose, the American flag, the Liberty Bell, and Uncle Sam.
28. Answers should include some of the following: portrait of Abraham Lincoln, a date, the word *Liberty*, the motto In God We Trust (front); and picture of the Lincoln Memorial, the words *One Cent* and *United States of America*, and the motto *E Pluribus Unum* (back).

29. She did not think she had done anything wrong. Susan B. Anthony was standing up for what she believed.
30. Answers will vary from state to state.
31. Answers should include one of the following: Sumatra, Borneo, Java, Celebes, Timor.
32. Answers will vary but may include more experience and knowledge.
33. six zeros
34. Answers will vary.
35. Answers will vary but should describe a local celebration.
36. Rome, Italy, on the continent of Europe
37. the male ruler of a county and its people; the female ruler of a county and its people
38. Silver is expensive and it cost too much to make the coins using silver.
39. Answers may include radio, television, newspapers, computers, and talking with other people.
40. Answers may include wood, brick, stone, concrete, stucco, and adobe.
41. northern South America
42. Answers will vary.
43. Answers will vary but may include veterinarian, nurse, engineer, accountant, architect, and teacher.
44. Democrats and Republicans
45. Answers may include that it is sometimes hard to look different; tall children may be perceived as being older while shorter children may be perceived as being younger; height may be an advantage in certain sports.
46. Salt Lake City, Utah; Denver, Colorado; Phoenix, Arizona; Santa Fe, New Mexico
47. Answers will vary but may include old buildings; the Atlantic Ocean; the Matanzas and San Sebastian Rivers; and Castillo de San Marcos (the oldest masonry fort in the continental United States).

48. Answers may include that some people still live in rural areas far from large department stores or shopping malls; people may be unable to drive; people may have an illness or disability that makes shopping difficult; people may like the convenience of shopping at home.
49. Answers may include that good relationships with other countries are important for trade, security, tourism, and sharing of knowledge and information.
50. Answers will vary.
51. Lake Erie and Lake Ontario
52. Answers may include Henry Hudson (England, Hudson Bay), Juan Ponce de Leon (Spain, Florida), or Jacques Cartier (France, Canada).
53. 1¢, 5¢, 10¢, 25¢, 50¢, and $1.00
54. Answers will vary but may include the Washington Monument, the Lincoln Memorial, the Capitol, the Smithsonian Institution, and so on.
55. Answers will vary.
56. the United States and Mexico
57. Answers will vary but may include explorers such as Jacques Marquette, Daniel Boone, Meriwether Lewis, or William Clark.
58. Advertisements are designed to create or increase the demand for a product.
59. We have laws to provide safety and security.
60. Answers will vary.
61. Mt. McKinley
62. Answers may include names like Baker, Shepherd, and so on.
63. income, spending, saving
64. citizens who are 18 years old and registered to vote
65. Answers will vary.
66. Answers will vary.
67. Answers will vary.
68. checks, debit cards, credit cards
69. The stars stand for the 50 states; the stripes stand for the original 13 colonies.

70. Answers will vary. One answer is that Texans are known for wearing cowboy boots and hats.
71. Sahara
72. Answers will vary.
73. All three have the motto In God We Trust and the word *Liberty*.
74. Answers will vary.
75. Answers may include the Empire State Building in New York, the John Hancock Building in Chicago, and so on.
76. Toronto is a natural port, and therefore an easy place for people to travel to by water.
77. Answers may include pans, cooking utensils, parts in automobiles, appliances, and so on.
78. to prevent people from making counterfeit, or fake, money
79. Answers will vary.
80. Dress for women is much more casual than in the 1800s. Women often wear slacks. They wear shorter skirts too.

81. Antarctica, Africa, Asia, Australia, Europe, North America, South America
82. The Red Cross is an international organization that cares for the sick and wounded in wartime and for those affected by natural disasters.
83. Having an allowance can teach you how to budget your money, how to save money, and how to make good choices about how to spend your money.
84. Answers will vary.
85. Answers will vary.
86. District of Columbia
87. Answers may include wood, brick, stucco, cement block, steel and glass, and so on.
88. You can save money in a bank, borrow money from a bank, or keep valuables in a bank.
89. With a secret ballot, no one knows who or what you voted for.
90. Answers will vary but may include baseball, basketball, football, and soccer.

91. Southern Hemisphere
92. Answers will vary.
93. Mexico, other Latin American countries, and the Phillipines
94. Answers might include sales tax.
95. Answers will vary but may include states such as Michigan and Illinois, cities such as Chicago, and so on.
96. Atlantic, Pacific, Indian, Arctic
97. Navy, Air Force, Marines
98. A mint makes coins.
99. Answers will vary.
100. Answers will vary.
101. Possible answers include Eastern Standard, Central Standard, Mountain Standard, Pacific Standard, Alaska Standard, and Hawaii-Aleutian.
102. 9
103. Answers may include the fact that the European countries are relatively small, and people probably travel from country to country often. Using the same currency would make trade and travel easier.
104. Answers will vary with each election.
105. Answers will vary.
106. Answers will vary.
107. Sacramento
108. Answers may include Germany, Japan, and Sweden.
109. Answers will vary but may include some of these: riding on the right side of the street, using hand signals, having proper lights and reflectors, having a bicycle license, and wearing a helmet.
110. Answers will vary.
111. Answers will vary.
112. Answers will vary depending on the President. George W. Bush was the governor of Texas before becoming President. Before that, he was a managing partner of the Texas Rangers baseball club.

113. Answers may include the business section of the newspapaer, or specific Internet sites.
114. Wyoming, Idaho, and Montana
115. Answers will vary but may include VCRs, DVDs, video games, and computer games.
116. Michigan, Indiana, Kentucky, West Virginia, and Pennsylvania
117. as of 2001, 34¢
118. Answers will vary but may include that both are very large states and both have climates and land good for farming.
119. The responsibilities of good citizenship include obeying the laws of the country, paying taxes, and voting in elections.
120. Answers will vary.
121. Maryland, West Virginia, Kentucky, Tennessee, and North Carolina
122. Another word for *bison* is *buffalo.* A bison is a large, four-legged wild animal of North America. It has a big, shaggy head and a hump on its shoulders.

123. That issue is probably scarce, so buyers might be willing to pay a lot for it.
124. Answers will vary but may include seatbelt laws, airbag laws, restrictions on new drivers, and so on.
125. Answers will vary.
126. Answers will vary. Atlantic side cities may include Jacksonville, Daytona, or Miami, among others. Gulf side cities may include Naples, Fort Myers, St. Petersburg, or Tampa, among others.
127. National Association for the Advancement of Colored People
128. import
129. Answers may include that he dosen't like the noise, or the fuss, among others.
130. Answers will vary.
131. Answers should include three of the following: NH, VT, MA, CT, NY, NJ, PA, MD, WV, VA, TN, NC.
132. Costa Rica and Columbia

133. *Credit* is trust in someone's ability and intention to pay. When someone uses a credit card to buy something, the store gives the cardholder the merchandise. At a later date the buyer gets a bill for the amount of the purchase and pays it then.
134. the Vice-President
135. Answers will vary.
136. Answers will vary but may include tornadoes, earthquakes, volcanic eruptions, blizzards, dust storms, and so on.
137. San Francisco Bay
138. Answers might include stop lights, community centers, road maintenance, and so on.
139. Answers will vary but may include the United States flag, the United States seal, the Liberty Bell, and the Statue of Liberty.
140. Answers may include crossword puzzles, other kinds of word puzzles, comic strips, movie or television reviews, and so on.
141. Kentucky
142. Mr. Alfred Nobel invented and manufactured dynamite. He left his fortune to establish the Nobel prizes.
143. Answers will vary.
144. By mail or door-to-door; may vary by 2010 census.
145. Arizona
146. Answers will vary.
147. Answers will vary but may include putting the first man on the moon, space shuttle flights, landing exploratory equipment on Mars, building a space station along with other nations.
148. services
149. England
150. Answers may include some other English-speaking countries but should include the United States and England.
151. Answers will vary.
152. Illinois

153. George Washington
154. to enforce the laws
155. Nashville
156. Asia
157. for refusing to give up her seat on the bus to a white person and thus sparking the Montgomery Bus Boycott
158. A reaper harvests grain.
159. Washington, D.C.
160. electronic
161. Lake Michigan
162. Henry Ford was an early car manufacturer. He is known for using an assembly line process to make cars. He made cars affordable for the average consumer.
163. Strauss's product was successful because there was a demand for sturdy pants.
164. A park district builds and maintains parks and runs recreational programs.
165. Answers will vary.
166. Locks on a seaway are chambers that are used to change the water level to raise or lower a ship.
167. A cattle drive is the movement of a large herd of cattle from one location to another.
168. Advertising is supposed to inform the consumer of the qualities of a product. It also often serves the purpose of creating a demand for a product.
169. a group of advisors chosen by the President
170. A subway is a train that runs underground.
171. California
172. Answers will vary.
173. Answers will vary. Students might tell of differences in price depending on time of show or difference in price depending on age of viewer.
174. National Aeronautics and Space Administration
175. movie cameras, video cameras, digital cameras

176. Answers may include Arizona, New Mexico, Texas, or Oklahoma.
177. World War II, Korean War, Vietnam War, Gulf War
178. American eagle
179. *Allegiance* means loyalty to a country or government.
180. in movie theaters or at home on VCR or DVD players